A Pet's Life

Hamsters

Anita Ganeri

Heinemann
LIBRARY

www.heinemann.co.uk/library

Visit our website to find out more information about **Heinemann Library** books.

To order:

☎ Phone 44 (0) 1865 888066

📄 Send a fax to 44 (0) 1865 314091

💻 Visit the Heinemann Bookshop at www.heinemann.co.uk/library to browse our catalogue and order online.

First published in Great Britain by Heinemann Library, Halley Court, Jordan Hill, Oxford OX2 8EJ, part of Harcourt Education.
Heinemann is a registered trademark of Harcourt Education Ltd.

Editorial: Jilly Attwood and Claire Throp
Design: Richard Parker and Tinstar Design Limited (www.tinstar.co.uk)
Picture Research: Rosie Garai
Production: Séverine Ribierre

Originated by Dot Gradations
Printed and bound in China by South China Printing Company

ISBN 0 431 17763 5
07 06 05 04 03
10 9 8 7 6 5 4 3 2 1

British Library Cataloguing in Publication Data
Ganeri, Anita
    Hamsters – (A Pet's Life)
    636.9'356
A full catalogue record for this book is available from the British Library.

Acknowledgements
The publishers would like to thank the following for permission to reproduce photographs: Alamy Images **p. 7**; Ardea **p. 6** (I. R. Beames); Armitage Pet Care **p. 12**; Dorling Kindersley Images **pp. 4, 5**; Haddon Davies **pp. 9, 13, 14, 17, 18, 19, 20, 21, 23, 24, 25, 26, 27**; Oxford Scientific Films **p. 8** (Renee Stockdale/AA); Trevor Clifford **p. 22**; Tudor Photography **pp. 10, 11, 15, 16**

Cover photograph reproduced with permission of Getty Images/G. K. & Vikki Hart.

The publishers would like to thank Pippa Bush of the RSPCA for her assistance in the preparation of this book.

Every effort has been made to contact copyright holders of any material reproduced in this book. Any omissions will be rectified in subsequent printings if notice is given to the publishers.

Contents

Any words appearing in the text in bold,
like this, are explained in the Glossary.

What is a hamster?

Hamsters make very good pets. The most popular type is the golden hamster. It gets its name from the colour of its fur.

There are many different kinds of hamsters.

Here you can see the different parts of a hamster's body and what each part is used for.

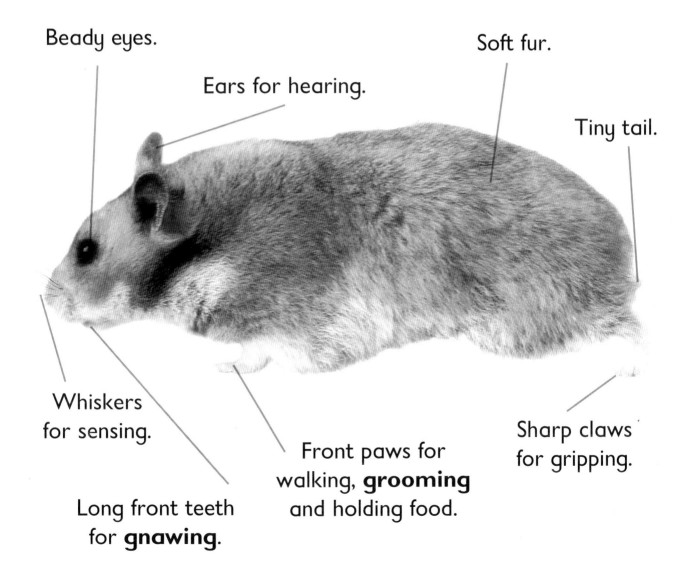

Beady eyes.

Ears for hearing.

Soft fur.

Tiny tail.

Whiskers for sensing.

Long front teeth for **gnawing**.

Front paws for walking, **grooming** and holding food.

Sharp claws for gripping.

Hamster babies

Baby hamsters are called **cubs**. A mother hamster has about five to seven cubs in a **litter**. The mother hamster feeds her cubs on milk.

Cubs are born with no fur and with their eyes closed.

The cubs are old enough to leave their mother when they are about six weeks old. Then they are ready to become pets.

At six weeks old, the cubs start to play and fight.

Your pet hamster

Hamsters are fun to keep as pets and are quite easy to look after. But you must be a good pet owner and care for your hamster properly.

You need time to feed your hamster, play with it and keep it clean.

If you go on holiday, make sure that someone looks after your hamster. It is best to take your hamster to a friend's house. Or ask someone to call in every day.

Your hamster must always have food, fresh water and clean bedding.

Choosing your hamster

You can buy a hamster from a good pet shop or from a hamster breeder. **Animal shelters** often have hamsters that need good homes.

Pick a lively hamster. A shy or nervous-looking hamster may not be very well.

Choose a plump hamster with soft, shiny fur. See that its skin is free from sores or bald patches. Check that its bottom is dry and clean.

A healthy hamster's eyes, ears, teeth, mouth and nose should be clean.

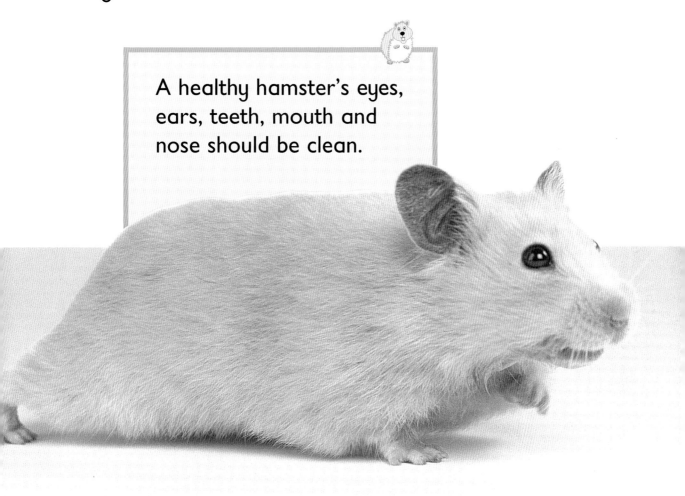

Fitting out your cage

Hamsters are very lively. They like to run and climb. Your hamster needs a large cage to live in, with a snug **nest box** inside to sleep in.

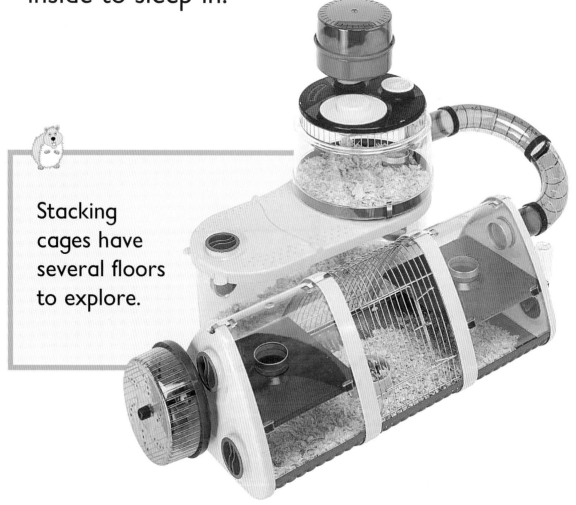

Stacking cages have several floors to explore.

The nest box in your hamster's cage should be filled with shredded tissue paper for bedding. Put the cage in a warm place but out of bright sunlight and away from draughts.

Put a layer of wood shavings on the floor of the cage.

Welcome home

You can bring your hamster home in a small cardboard box. At home, put your hamster in its cage. Leave it alone for a few hours to settle in.

Make sure the box has holes in it so that your hamster has air to breathe.

Be gentle when you pick up your hamster. Move slowly and quietly. Otherwise your hamster may get frightened and try to bite you.

To pick up your hamster, scoop it up gently with both hands.

Play time

Hamsters need lots of exercise. Put an exercise wheel in the cage. Jam jars, cardboard tubes and climbing frames also make good toys.

The exercise wheel must be solid so that your hamster does not trap its feet.

If you let your pet out of its cage, shut all the doors and windows. Hamsters can run very fast and are small and tricky to find.

Let your hamster climb from one of your hands to another.

Feeding time

Hamsters like to eat seeds, nuts and grains. You can buy a mixture from a pet shop. Hamsters like to store food in **pouches** in their cheeks. They eat it later.

You can also feed your hamster some fresh fruit and vegetables.

You should feed your hamster once a day in the evening. Put the food in a heavy dish so that it does not tip over.

Make sure that your pet always has fresh water to drink. Buy your hamster a **drip feeder**.

Cleaning the cage

You can help your hamster to stay healthy by keeping its cage clean. Every day, take away any **droppings** and bits of old food.

Wash out the food bowl
and **drip feeder** every day.

Every week, give the whole cage a thorough clean. Change the layer of wood shavings on the floor. Don't forget to wash your hands after cleaning your hamster's cage.

Put some fresh bedding in the **nest box**.

Growing up

Hamsters grow up very quickly. When a golden hamster is fully grown, it will measure about 10 cm long and weigh about 100 g.

A hamster can easily fit in your hands.

If you put two golden hamsters in the same cage, they may fight each other. Never keep a hamster in a cage with other animals.

Golden hamsters like to live on their own.

A healthy hamster

Your hamster will stay healthy if you care for it properly. But hamsters can catch colds and flu from people. A wet tail is another sign of illness.

If you think your hamster looks unwell, take it to a vet.

Your hamster's front teeth grow all the time. If its teeth grow too long, your hamster may not be able to eat properly.

Give your hamster a wooden **gnawing** block to wear its teeth down.

Old age

If you look after your hamster, it may live for about two to three years. As it gets older, it might lose some fur and put on weight.

An old hamster might need special care.

It can be very upsetting when your pet dies. Try not to be too sad. Just remember the happy times you shared together.

Caring for your hamster will help you learn how to treat animals properly.

Useful tips

- Hamsters wake up at night. So put the cage in a place where it will not disturb you.

- Don't wake your hamster up in the day to play. It might bite you.

- Keep the cage out of reach of cats and other pets.

- Hamsters clean their fur with their front paws. But you need to brush long-haired hamsters gently every day with a soft toothbrush.

- Don't line the cage with newspaper. The ink is **poisonous** to your hamster.

- Let your hamster sniff your fingers. It will get to know you by how you smell.

Fact file

- Wild hamsters live in the desert.

- Wild hamsters spend the day sleeping in **burrows** under the ground. This keeps them cool.

- All pet golden hamsters come from one family found in the desert in Syria in 1930.

- The name 'hamster' comes from a German word which means 'hoarder'. This is because hamsters **hoard** food in their cheeks.

- An adult hamster needs about 15 g of food a day. That's about a teaspoonful.

- Hamsters are short-sighted. They cannot see very well.

Glossary

burrows holes in the ground where wild hamsters live

cubs baby hamsters

drip feeder a bottle that lets water slowly drip out. It is fixed to the hamster's cage.

droppings hamsters' poo

gnawing chewing and biting

grooming gently brushing and cleaning your hamster's fur. Hamsters also groom themselves.

hoard store or keep for later

litter a group of hamster babies

nest box a box filled with bedding for your hamster to sleep in

poisonous something that can cause illness or death

pouches spaces in a hamster's cheeks where it stores food

More information

Books to read

First Pets: Hamsters, S. Meredith (Usborne Publishing, 1999)

How to Look After Your Hamster, Colin and Jacqui Hawkins (Walker Books, 1995)

My Pet: Hamsters and Gerbils, Honor Head (Belitha Press, 2000)

The Official RSPCA Pet Guide: Care for your Hamster (HarperCollins, 1990)

Websites

www.rspca.org.uk
   The website of the Royal Society for the Prevention of Cruelty to Animals in Britain.

www.pethealthcare.co.uk
   Information about keeping and caring for first pets.

www.petnet.com.au
   Information about being a good pet owner.

Index

Titles in the *A Pet's Life* series include:

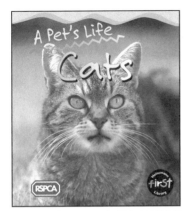

Hardback   0 431 17762 7

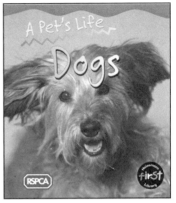

Hardback   0 431 17764 3

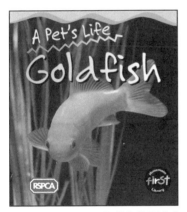

Hardback   0 431 17765 1

Hardback   0 431 17761 9

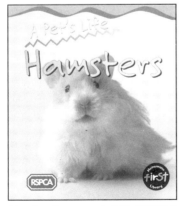

Hardback   0 431 17763 5

Hardback   0 431 17760 0

Find out about the other titles in this series on our website www.heinemann.co.uk/library